KHENPO TSEWANG GYATSO

THE HEALTHY MIND INTERVIEWS

KHENPO TSEWANG GYATSO

Henry M. Vyner, M.D.

Vajra Publications
Kathmandu, Nepal

Published by:
Vajra Publications
Jyatha, Kathmandu
e-mail: bidur_la@mos.com.np

ISBN 99933-695-8-6

Printed in Nepal

FOR
PEPPER

ACKNOWLEDGEMENTS

Thank you, once again, to Bidur Dongol for his excellent ideas -- including the idea of creating the Healthy Mind Interview Series.

Thank you to Ram Krishna Dongol and Shanti Dongol of Dongol Printers for their excellent ideas and selfless hard work on the design and layout of this book.

Thank you to Maureen Fry, Sarah Ralston and Alan Schaaf for their help in finding the cover photo. Thank you to Sarah Ralston for taking the photo itself.

Thank you to Pepper Black for editing and proofreading the manuscript.

Thank you most of all to Khenpo Tsewang Gyatso.

TABLE OF CONTENTS

INTRODUCTION

THE INTERVIEWS

APPENDIX

THE HEALTHY MIND INTERVIEWS

"Self Awareness is always bliss."
The Sixteenth Karmapa

This book is the inaugural volume in a series of books that we are calling "The Healthy Mind Interviews." The interviews contained in these books will describe the characteristics of the healthy and happy human mind as they have been known and experienced by Tibetan lamas. The lamas will also be talking about how one goes about cultivating a healthy mind.

The exciting thing about these interviews is that they are not, for the most part, abstract or philosophical discussions of the nature of the healthy mind. The lamas directly describe the characteristics of the healthy mind, and they do so by making reference to experiences of mind that we can all recognize from our own experiences with meditation and introspection.

For the last twelve years now I have been systematically interviewing Tibetan lamas about their experiences of their own mind in meditation for the purposes of:

(a) Developing a descriptive science of the stream of consciousness, and

(b) Using that descriptive science to construct a scientifically valid theory of the defining characteristics of the healthy human mind.

Each of the books in "The Healthy Mind Series" will present interviews that have been done with one specific lama.

The volume you hold in your hands contains excerpts from a series of interviews that were done with the Bön lama Khenpo Nyima Wangyal. The next volume will present the thoughts of the Nyingma lama Khenpo Tsewang Gyatso. The third volume will present interviews that have been done with the Bhutanese lama Lopon Tegchoke, and so forth.

These last twelve years of lama interviews have been interesting. One of the main reasons I took up the task of doing this research is that most societies misunderstand the nature of the healthy mind. Almost all societies operate on the assumption that a healthy mind is a mind with a strong ego. As a result, we cause ourselves to suffer and to fight with ourselves and other human beings.

The Tibetans, in contrast, believe that a healthy mind is a mind with no ego – given the paradox that you have to have an ego to be egoless, and they actually possess an eleven centuries old science of the stream of consciousness that seems to scientifically prove that their position is correct.

Throughout the history of Buddhism, meditation has always been used to do two fundamentally different things. First and foremost, meditation is the primary tool that Buddhists have used to cultivate egoless, or nondual, mind. Secondly, meditation has also been the instrument that Buddhists have used to empirically study the workings of the mind.

Meditation is a perfect tool for empirically studying the mind because it creates a situation in which the mind is able to know and observe itself. Think about it for a moment. There are literally hundreds of different kinds of meditation techniques, but no matter what technique you use when you meditate, or for that matter introspect, your mind becomes aware of itself. The mind is both the subject and object of the experiences created by meditation.

When the mind knows itself in this dualistic mode of experience,[1] sometimes it seems as though there are actually two different minds present within that experience. There is one mind, the stream of consciousness, that presents meanings to the mind's awareness, and then there is a second mind – the awareness that knows and responds to those meanings.[2]

The stream of consciousness presents meanings to the watcher in the form of thoughts, images, feelings and emotions, and the watcher can and does respond to these meanings in a number of different ways. For example, the watcher might repress an emotion, hold onto a thought or do absolutely nothing at all.

Every single response that the watcher makes to a given meaning initiates a causal sequence that determines the fate of that meaning. Different responses cause different things to occur. For example, when the watcher represses or attaches an emotion, that emotion will remain present in awareness as a mood. When the watcher judges an individual moment of consciousness, it will have dual, as opposed to non-dual, awareness of that moment of consciousness. And so forth.

Meditation makes it possible to observe all of these processes. Over the centuries, meditation has been the mental microscope that Buddhists have used to make systematic observations of the stream of consciousness. These observations were made for the very real purpose of developing a body of knowledge that could be used to both understand the nature of the mind and guide the practice of meditation. After all, Buddhists practice meditation for the very real and serious purpose of changing the way their mind works. In an endeavor of this sort, you want to understand the consequences of what you are doing.

The DzogChen[3] traditions of Tibet[4] have, for the most part, focused on making systematic observations of the processes by which the mind knows and controls itself. These observations, and the theory they have generated, have become, over the centuries, a comprehensive body of knowledge about the mind. This body of knowledge contains understandings of the mind that modern scientific psychology simply does not yet possess.

Amongst many other things, this DzogChen science of the mind seems to have empirically understood two fundamental things:

(1) The defining characteristics, or nature, of the healthy human mind.

(2) How to cultivate a healthy human mind.

Let me just say briefly that this Tibetan mind science is not, at first glance, a science in our modern sense of the scientific endeavor. For one, the Tibetans who developed this mind science did not think of themselves as scientists. Nor were they familiar with our notions of either science or the scientific method. Furthermore, their observations of the mind were and are often presented in symbolic religious language. Nonetheless, they were scientists.

They were scientists in the sense that they made systematic observations of a group of phenomena, and then derived, from these observations, theories about those phenomena. They used the sixth sense, which is called the mental consciousness in Buddhist psychology, and the mind's eye in our own parlance, to make observations of the phenomena that appear in and as the stream of consciousness. They then used these observations to construct systematic theories of the healthy and unhealthy human mind.

In the lama interviews that I have been fortunate enough to do over these last twelve years, the lamas and I have been discussing this DzogChen science of the mind at great length. We have done so by talking about their experiences of their own minds in meditation, and by talking about the conclusions they have drawn from those experiences.

In having these discussions, we have actually been developing a descriptive and theoretical science of the processes by which the mind knows and transforms itself. This science has existed for centuries in the DzogChen traditions of Tibet, and in our interviews, we are putting this knowledge into modern scientific form.

As such, the interviews being presented in this series of books are scientific documents. They are scientific documents in the sense that they contain an immense amount of empirical knowledge about the mind.

They are also spiritual documents. They contain knowledge of the mind that will help a person understand their own mind, the nature of the healthy mind and how to cultivate a healthy mind.

Ultimately, a careful reading of these interviews will lead you to the understanding that one practices meditation for the para-doxical purpose of trying to cultivate a state of mind in which you do nothing without trying to do nothing. The egoless mind is a mind that leaves itself in its natural state.

Footnotes

1 The mind can have both dual and nondual awareness of itself.

2 By meaning, I mean any construct that the mind creates to elaborate upon, or give meaning to, its sensory experience. Meanings appear in the stream of consciousness as thoughts, emotions, images feelings and so forth.

3 All of the spellings of Tibetan words in this book are phonetic spellings.

4 There are two DzogChen traditions in Tibet. One is found in the Nyingma lineage of Tibetan Buddhism. The second one is found in the Bön religion – the indigenous religion of the Tibetan plateau.

KHENPO TSEWANG GYATSO

"On the DzogChen path you don't reject thoughts. When a negative thought arises, you just recognize it and let it dissolve."

Khenpo Tsewang Gyatso graduated first in his class at the Harvard of Tibetan monastic universities; so there can be no doubt he has a keen intellect. More than that, he is a man who is defined by his erudition. He is, after all, a professor of Buddhist Studies at one of the great monastic universities of the Tibetan diaspora, and as the following interviews will show, he is comfortable with and quick to use the language and categories of Buddhist philosophy.

But if you ask his students about the Khenpo – the Tibetan monks who study with him at Namdroling Monastery, the first very thing they will always tell you about Khenpo Tsewang is that he is a man of great compassion. And in my experience, it is true. He is, to be sure, a man who is defined by his scholarship, but he is also a man of stunning and unremitting compassion. Khenpo Tsewang is, by all accounts, a very generous human being.

Khenpo Tsewang Gyatso was born in the Lhodrak Valley of south central Tibet in 1954. The Lhodrak Valley is adjacent to Tibet's border with the kingdom of Bhutan, and the valley straddles the traditional trading route that lies between the two countries.

In 1962, in the early stages of the harsh Chinese occupation of Tibet, Khenpo Tsewang left Tibet with his family. Like so many other Tibetan people at that time in history, Khenpo Tsewang's family literally walked out of Tibet through the high passes of the Himalaya.

On arriving in India, Khenpo Tsewang was sent to a government school in Darjeeling in the Indian state of West Bengal, where he excelled as a student. While there, he became a monk at the age of ten.

In 1969, Khenpo Tsewang matriculated at the Central Institute of Higher Tibetan Studies which is located in the village of Sarnath, just outside the sacred Hindu city of Varanasi. It was here that his career as a scholar really began. As a student at the Institute, he took up the serious study of the seminal works of Buddhist philosophy.

Khenpo Tsewang says that there have been three Buddhist texts that have profoundly shaped his views of life. It was at the Central Institute that Khenpo Tsewang studied the first of these texts: Mipham's "Beacon of Certainty," which is a commentary on the ninth chapter of another book: Santideva's "Bodhicharyavatara." The "Bodhicharyavatara" is the definitive text on how to pursue the practice of Buddhism towards the end of becoming a Bodhisattva.[1]

In the study of Tibetan Buddhism, there are famous chapters, chapters that are studied over and over again because they are crucial to understanding a particular issue. The ninth chapter of the "Bodhicharyavatara" is one of those chapters, and it is a discussion of the central idea of Buddhist philosophy and psychology – emptiness. Emptiness is the ultimate reality of Buddhism. Tibetan practitioners spend years and decades trying to: (1) intellectually understand emptiness and (2) realize direct experiences of emptiness. These are two very different tasks.

Mipham was an important Nyingma[2] scholar of emptiness who lived in the late nineteenth century. Before Mipham, the fourteenth century Gelugpa[3] scholar-lama Tsongkhapa had formulated the definitive Tibetan understandings of emptiness. Mipham's place in history is that he formulated an understanding of emptiness that expanded upon Tsongkhapa's work by reconciling the notion of emptiness to the Nyingma experience of meditation.

By studying and taking to heart Mipham's "Beacon of Certainty," Khenpo Tsewang aligned himself with the Bodhisattva tradition of Mahayana Buddhism and addressed its deepest issues. In Khenpo's words, "The "Beacon of Certainty" was important to him because it explained "the absolute true nature of phenomena and connected that understanding to both the sutras and the tantras."

At a later point in his life, Khenpo studied a second text that was essential in developing his understanding of emptiness: The "Guhyagarbha Tantra." Khenpo studied the Guhyagharba with Dilgo Khyentse Rinpoche in Nepal, and Dilgo Khyentse became one of Khenpo's two root lamas.[4]

Khenpo Tsewang went on to graduate first in his class at the Central Institute of Buddhist studies in 1978, and for that accomplishment he received a special award from His Holiness the Dalai Lama.

After his graduation, he received an invitation to teach at Palyul Namdroling Monastery in southern India. In the aftermath of the Tibetan exodus to India from Tibet, the Indian government created a number of Tibetan refugee settlements in southern India. Namdroling Monastery is located in one of those settlements – Bylakuppe.

The head lama of Namdroling is Penor Rinpoche, and Penor Rinpoche is Khenpo Tsewang's second root lama. Penor Rinpoche is one of the three great lamas with whom Khenpo Tsewang has studied DzogChen meditation. The other two lamas are Nyoshul Khen Rinpoche and Khenpo Jigme Phuntsok.

During his early years at Bylakuppe, Khenpo studied Longchenpa's "Kindly Bent to Ease Us" – which is the third text he holds dear. He studied "Kindly Bent to Ease Us" with Nyoshul Khen Rinpoche. In Khenpo Tsewang's words, he values the text because it "explains about the true nature of mind."

Khenpo Tsewang remains at Namdroling Monastery to this day, although he now spends much of his time travelling and teaching in the West. He was elevated to the position of Khenpo in 1983, and more recently he was elevated to the position of Khenchen – a great Khenpo.

I first met and interviewed Khenpo Tsewang Gyatso at Namdroling Monastery in March of 1997. At that time, I interviewed the Khenpo five times, and since then, I have had the good fortune to interview him three more times at his sister Ugyen's house in northern California.

THE INTERVIEW

The central, but by no means the only, issue of these interviews is this question: What is the nature of the healthy human mind? The Buddhist tradition, as a whole, takes the position that a healthy and happy mind is an egoless mind – given the paradox that you have to have an ego to be egoless. The DzogChen tradition to which Khenpo Tsewang belongs has developed a science of the mind that empirically demonstrates that this hypothesis is correct.

Khenpo Tsewang begins the interview by making the case that the mind with an ego is not a healthy mind. He goes on to discuss exactly what the ego is and how it causes, in his words, "all human suffering." Again, in his words, "The whole complete point about the ego is that it is never satisfied. The ego never feels it has enough money, enough wealth or enough happiness."

The Khenpo then goes on to describe the ego as it is experienced within the mind, and his descriptions will make it possible for you to recognize exactly what is and is not ego in your own mind. It is essential, when trying to cultivate the egoless mind, to be able to confidently discern the difference between your egocentric and egoless mind; the difference between dual and nondual mind.

After discussing the ego, Khenpo moves on to describe the experience of Rigpa – the awareness that is the egoless mind. He tells us several different things about rigpa:

(1) How Rigpa relates to the thoughts and emotions that appear in the stream of consciousness.

(2) The type of awareness that Rigpa has of the meanings that appear in its stream of consciousness.

(3) The qualities, or characteristics, of the awareness that is Rigpa.

(4) The process by which Rigpa is developed, and

(5) How to recognize when you have experienced Rigpa.

The final portion of the book is an appendix. The appendix contains a long passage in which Khenpo Tsewang discusses the integration of the DzogChen and Bodhisattva paths. For reasons that you will find considered at length in this passage, the two paths appear to be contradictory, but the Khenpo clearly shows – by once again describing the relevant states of mind, how the two paths are integrated with one another.

Footnotes

1 In a general sense, a Bodhisattva is someone who is very advanced on the Buddhist path, and who has, in particular, a well developed sense of compassion. Technically, a bodhisattva is a person who has successfully developed bodhicitta – which is usually translated as the "mind of enlightenment." There are two kinds of bodhicitta: relative and absolute. Relative bodhicitta is the genuine aspiration to free all human beings from suffering. Absolute bodhicitta is the fully enlightened mind that knows the emptiness of all phenomena.

2 The Nyingma tradition is one of the four sects, if you will, of Tibetan Buddhism. Kenpo Tsewang Gyatso is a Nyingma lama.

3 The Gelugpa tradition is another one of the four sects of Tibetan Buddhism.

4 In general, a student of Tibetan Buddhism studies with many different lamas. You might take a class from one lama, study several different texts with many more lamas and study meditation with yet several other lamas. A person's root lama is the lama that is most important to a practitioner and the primary guide of that student's development.

THE INTERVIEW

THE EGOCENTRIC MIND IS
NOT A HEALTHY MIND

HMV: In the Western world, and in many other of the world's societies as well, people believe that a healthy mind is a mind with a strong ego. Do you think that a healthy mind is a mind with a strong ego?

KTG: No.

HMV: Why not?

KTG: Because the ego[1] pollutes the mind. It is actually the cause of problems, as opposed to being healthy. Because of the ego, all sorts of problems arise – attachment, aversion, negativity, anger, pride and all of the afflicted, or painful, minds.

HMV: Ok.

KTG: As Chandrakirti, Santideva[2] and many other teachers have said, all suffering and faults arise from the attachment to the self, or ego. And because we see things in this way, all practitioners – all of the yogis and yoginis – try to get rid of the ego. When there is no ego, when one is pure in one's nature, one can realize independence and freedom. And at the same time, one can still do anything that one wants to do in the real world.

HMV: It sounds like you are saying Khenpo that ego is actually the main cause of psychological suffering.

KTG: Yes, that's true.

HMV: And it sounds like one of the things you mean by suffering is that the ego causes painful emotions to arise.

KTG: Yes. Sure.

HMV: Is the arising of painful emotions the only form of suffering that ego causes? Or does it cause other forms of suffering as well?

KTG: Yes, there are other forms too. All forms of suffering are caused by the ego. The complete cause of getting rebirth in cyclic existence[3] is the result of being attached to, or holding onto, the ego. Dag-dzin. The grasping of "I." When you are born into samsara, or cyclic existence, the ego and its pride makes us want to gain fame, wealth and prosperity; and when there is any kind of obstacle to having them, it gives rise to all sorts of emotions, depression and suffering.

HMV: It sounds like you are saying that ego is the cause of all psychological suffering.

KTG: Yes. Yes. (Emphatically)

HMV: It also sounds like you are saying that the mind with an ego is not a happy or healthy mind at all.

KTG: The mind with an ego is neither a happy mind nor a healthy mind. That's true in two ways: relatively and absolutely. Normally, in the relative world, people think, "Oh I'm good. I'm rich. I'm healthy. I'm fine." Then people think, "Oh I have a healthy mind; a healthy body. Because of that I'm happy, wealthy and good." Relatively, it seems like this, but at the same time there are so many problems. To really experience ultimate happiness, or just even peace, to really have that healthy or happy mind, that can only happen when one gets rid of the ego.

HMV: Yes, and I'd like to come back to the egoless mind in a moment, but first I'd like to pursue this notion of the ego a little bit further with you. It's true. A lot of people would say, "Look, if I have a lot of money and I'm famous, then I'm happy." But it sounds like you are saying no; that's not necessarily the case. That if a person has fame and fortune, that actually they won't be happy.

KTG: Yes. They won't necessarily be happy.

HMV: Why is that?

KTG: Because when you have an ego, there is no satisfaction. The whole complete point about the ego is that it is never satisfied. The ego never feels it has enough money, enough wealth or enough happiness. One never really gets satisfied. Still you want more and more. In that way, one never really gets satisfied. And then you live in fear of losing what you have. And you also suffer because you have enemies. Once ego loses fame or wealth, then there is double suffering. Ego increases your suffering because you have an unsatisfied mind. It is not a healthy mind.

HMV: If the pursuits of the ego do not provide happiness, would it be fair to say that real happiness, real satisfaction, is actually the joy that is the nature of the mind.[4]

KTG: Yes.

HMV: And that when you have ambition, the kind of ambition that comes with ego, that you don't get to experience the joy and peace that is the nature, or natural state, of the mind.

KTG: Yes. (Emphatic)

Annotation: In this last series of questions, Khenpo Tsewang is saying that genuine and lasting happiness is not achieved by the pursuits of the ego. Genuine happiness is attained by realizing the natural state of the mind, the nature of mind.

One of the central tenets of DzogChen mind science is that the mind has a natural state.

This natural state of the mind is the state that arises when the mind is not being altered by the ego.

In contrast, the egocentric, or socialized, mind is a mind that is forever and always trying to change itself. It changes itself as a means of controlling itself. The socialized mind controls itself because it is necessary for all people living in society to control their mind and behavior.

The egocentric mind controls itself by changing itself. It changes its thoughts, feelings and emotions so that they match its sense of identity. In using this approach to self control, the mind with an ego removes itself from its natural condition.

The egoless mind, in contrast, controls itself by leaving itself in its natural state. The mind that is left in its natural state has a number of different healthy characteristics. One of those healthy characteristics is that it abides in a state of joy. This joy appears spontaneously when the mind leaves itself in its natural state.

The analogy of the sun and clouds is often used to explain this idea. The sun is always present in our sky and solar system. It is, of course, there even when we can't see it because it has been covered over by clouds. In much the same way, the natural joy of the mind is always present within the mind, but sometimes it appears as though it is not there because it has been covered over by the thoughts and emotions created by the ego.

DEFINITION OF EGO

HMV: For the sake of clarity, let's develop a definition of the ego, and let's start by taking a look at the Tibetan term for ego – "dag dzin." What does the word "dag" mean? And what does the word "dzin" mean?

KTG: Dag is the existence of phenomena.

HMV: Is it the belief that all phenomena have a self?

KTG: Yes. There are two types of ego. There is the grasping of one's own person, and then there is the grasping of all other phenomena. These are the two main categories of ego.[5] The deluded mind, the mind that has an ego, thinks that it is a person that has a self, or personality, that has a true existence.

HMV: Are you saying that the mind with an ego thinks that it has a permanent identity of some sort?

KTG: Yes. A person is actually just the five aggregates,[6] which are the basis of the self. It is onto these aggregates, that one imputes the self.

HMV: So a human being is actually composed of many different physical and mental elements, and if you think you have a permanent self, or dag, what you are actually doing is attributing a concept of self to the elements of your mind and body.

KTG: Yes.

HMV: So philosophically, this is what the word "dag" means.

KTG: Yes. Dag is the inherent existence of a self. It is a strong concept, a grasping, that makes us think that we have a self, a truly existing self.

HMV: Let's try to bring that to life a bit. Would that be the same as me saying "I am a doctor; and I am always a doctor no matter what the circumstances. Even when I'm at home, or when I'm in Tibet. And more than that, I'm a good doctor; always a good doctor." Is this what you mean by dag? Is it some kind of concept of one's self like that?

KTG: Yes. Normally you just think I'm Doctor Hank. I am. When someone says Doctor Hank, you automatically have the response, "This is me." This is the self. We have that same sense of I when we say, "I am going. I am good. I am talking to you. I want to do this. Today I feel sick." These are all communications within the relative life in which we use that "I."

Ego is that sense of "I" plus pride, which is a type of grasping by the ego. There is a Santideva text in which he says that ego also includes thinking you are better than other people.

HMV: That's part of the "I" too.

KTG: Yes. And there is also a feeling of inferiority that is part of ego, as well. Compared to this other person, I am inferior. That is also part of the ego, or self.

HMV: So the first element of ego is some kind of "I am;" some kind of concept of whom you are.

KTG: Yes.

HMV: The second element is comparing your self and thinking you are better than other people.

KTG: Yes.

HMV: The third element is thinking you are not as good as other people.

KTG: Yes. One sort of humiliates one self. One just sort of thinks, "Oh compared to this other person I'm just not so good."

HMV: So those are the three main elements of "dag."

KTG: Yes.

HMV: Now what about the word "dzin"? What is the grasping aspect of ego all about?

KTG: "Dzin" means grasping. To grasp something is to attribute a concept to it. In the case of a person, it's the concept with which you impute an "I" or an ego to the five skandhas. Of course in reality, not just in absolute reality, even in the relative sense, if you really investigate what this "I" is, it does not really exist at all. So we end up grasping, or clinging to, this concept of "I" that we create. Even in our dreams, when you have a nightmare, you just think "Oh I'm being chased by something." You get scared. This is grasping, clinging, to the self you have imputed to the five skandhas. So that grasping is actually ignorance.

HMV: Who is grasping? And what is being grasped?

KTG: What is being grasped is the "I", your concept of your self, and it is one's self who is doing the grasping. It is based mainly within one's mind.

HMV: In other words, it happens in the mind.

KTG: Yes.

HMV: Let's see if we can talk about this in terms of the actual experience of the mind.

KTG: Ok.

HMV: My experience when I meditate, and I think it's the same for most people, is that in the dual experience of mind, not the nondual experience of mind, just the dual experience...

KTG: Yes.

HMV: It seems like there is a watcher, an awareness, that is watching the stream of consciousness.

KTG: Yes.

HMV: It's just like standing on the side of a river and watching the river flow by.

KTG: Yes. (Emphatic)

HMV: Except in this case, there is an awareness, which we are calling the watcher, that is watching the stream of consciousness go by.

KTG: Yes.

HMV: It seems to me that the essence of ego is just this: The ego is actually the watcher in those moments when it grasps the meanings – the thoughts and emotions – that appear in its stream of consciousness.

KTG: Ok.

HMV: The yulchen, the egocentric watcher, is a watcher that grasps thoughts and emotions. For example, one way it grasps thoughts is by rejecting them.

KTG: Ok.

HMV: Another way it grasps thoughts is by accepting them.

KTG: Ok.

HMV: And finally, the watcher is grasping thoughts and emotions whenever it follows them, jay-soo-drong.[7]

KTG: Yes. (Emphatically)

HMV: Would you agree that these different forms of grasping are the essence of ego? Or would you disagree with that?

KTG: That is ok in a way. But when you accept, reject or follow, that is also a thought.

HMV: Most definitely.

KTG: And that thought is not separate from your watcher, your mind.

HMV: So the watcher is the awareness that is watching the stream of consciousness, and the watcher is actually a thought.

KTG: Yes.

HMV: And it sounds like you are also saying that when the watcher grasps something, that it is just one thought grasping another thought.

KTG: Yes. Grasping is an action of the mind that arises as a thought. It is like the waves and the ocean. The watcher, or yulchen, is the subject and the thoughts are the objects that are being grasped.

HMV: Ok. Could we say, then, that the mechanism by which the mind creates a concept of it self is one in which one thought grasps another thought? Is the self created when one moment of mental consciousness grasps another moment of mental consciousness?

KTG: Yes, of course, the grasping of self is the action of a moment of mental consciousness.

Annotation: In these last passages, we have been considering two different but related definitions of ego. Khenpo Tsewang started off by giving us a philosophical definition of ego. He said, in his discussion of the five skandhas, that people see themselves as having an ego when their mind grasps, or attributes a concept of identity to, the elements of which their mind and body are composed.

I then asked Khenpo to consider an empirical, or psychological, version of his definition. I suggested that the ego is created when the mind grasps, or attributes a concept of identity to, itself. To be more specific, the ego is created and recreated in every moment in which the mind's awareness, or watcher, attributes a concept of identity to its thoughts and emotions. In other words, the ego actually is, and can be defined as, a specific mode of self awareness. It is a mode of self awareness in which the mind has conceptual, or dual, awareness of itself. As we will be seeing, the mind has more than one type of self awareness.

KTG: The stream of consciousness carries on all sorts of thoughts and also holds all sorts of habitual tendencies.

HMV: By habitual tendencies, do you mean the bag-chags?[8]

KTG: Yes. Bag-chags. All sorts of actions.

HMV: And just to be clear, are you saying that the bag-chags actually appear in the stream of consciousness?

KTG: Yes.

HMV: Do individual thoughts appear in the stream of consciousness?

KTG: Yes.

HMV: Do emotions appear in the stream of consciousness?

KTG: Yes.

HMV: Could we take a moment and say exactly what the bag-chags are and how they appear in the stream of consciousness? Are bag-chags recurring patterns of thought that appear over and over again in the stream of consciousness?

KTG: Yes. This is true, but we should also mention that there are both gross and subtle levels of bag-chags.

HMV: What is the difference between gross and subtle bag-chags?

KTG: Subtle bag-chags are a potential in the mind stream that gives rise to the habitual tendencies. The gross bag-chags, or habitual thoughts, are what you really do. They are the actions that appear in the stream of consciousness.

HMV: Now when I look at my own bag-chags, the recurring patterns of thoughts that appear in my own mind, it looks to me like they are telling stories.

KTG: Yes.

HMV: It also seems to me that they are telling the same stories over and over again. Would it be correct to say that, in general, the bag-chags are stories that the mind repeats to itself over and over again?

KTG: Yes.

HMV: Secondly, when I look at the content of these recurring stories, it looks to me like they are just ego. They are ego in the sense that they are stories created by my mind to support my concept of self. Would you agree?

KTG: Oh yes.

HMV: Is that their purpose? To delude a person into thinking that their ego is real?

KTG: Yes. That is also bag-chags.

HMV: Is that their purpose?

KTG: On the level of relative truth, they have that purpose. But if we are thinking of liberation, looking for peace and happiness, then there is no purpose. They just create more problems.

Annotation: Bag-chags are one of the more important discoveries of theoretical and applied Buddhist psychology. To develop an egoless, or healthy, mind it is of the utmost importance to: (1) recognize the recurring patterns of thought that are present in your own mind and (2) refrain from believing, or getting caught up in, the stories they tell.

In essence, a bag-chags is a recurring thought pattern that appears in your mind as a repetitive stream of thoughts and emotions. When you meditate, it is only too easy to see these recurring thoughts. They appear as cycles of thoughts that tell the same story over and over again. This is what Khenpo Tsewang is calling the gross bag-chags.

The egocentric mind believes and lives in the narratives created by the gross bag-chags; and it does so because these narratives support its sense of identity. The egoless mind, in contrast, does not believe and/or live in these ego narratives. It allows the gross bag-chags to remain in their natural state, and as a result, they dissolve into and become the nondual nature of mind that they have always been.

Gross bag-chags are empirical, or observable, phenomena. Subtle bag-chags, in contrast, are a theoretical entity. In Buddhist psychology, the existence of subtle bag-chags has been inferred from the observation of the gross bag-chags – the habitual patterns of thought. The subtle bag-chag is thought of as being: (1) a structural deposit in a person's stream of consciousness that is (2) the source of one specific habitual pattern of thought, or gross bag-chag. To my eye, the "subtle bag-chag" of Buddhist psychology is very similar to the "fixed unconscious idea" (idée fixe) of western psychology.[9]

EGO IS THE WATCHER
THAT GRASPS

HMV: Now let's back up for a moment. I was making the case before that the defining essence of the ego is the actions of the watcher. By actions, I mean the behaviors by which the watcher holds onto its concept of self: the behaviors of accepting, rejecting and following the thoughts and emotions that appear in its stream of consciousness. Do you think that this is the essence of ego? Or do you think that it's something else?

KTG: When you say watcher, watcher is only a word that you apply to somebody. But who is that watcher? Can you really point out the watcher?

HMV: I'd like to try, once again, to see if we can talk about these issues in terms of the actual experience of the mind.

KTG: Ok.

HMV: Once again, the mind's dual experience of itself in meditation is one in which it seems as though there is a watcher, or awareness, that is watching the stream of consciousness.

KTG: Yes.

HMV: In my experience, the awareness that watches the stream of consciousness seems to have two different states. It has two states in the sense that it has two different ways of knowing and responding to the thoughts and emotions that appear in its stream of consciousness. To my eye, one of these states of self awareness is egocentric, and the other is egoless.

In the DzogChen tradition, the egocentric state is called the watcher, and the egoless state is called "Rigpa."

The egocentric watcher is defined by its perpetual attempts to change the stream of consciousness. It accepts and rejects thoughts and emotions; and it creates and lives in ego sustaining narratives that are recurring patterns of thought. These are the defining actions of the ego, and they are the means by which the watcher aligns the content of the meanings that appear in the stream of consciousness with its concept of self. This watcher is called "yulchen" in Tibetan, and in fact the word yulchen is translated into English as "the watcher."

KTG: Yes.

HMV: On the other hand, the mind's awareness is egoless when that awareness is rigpa.[10] Rigpa, unlike the watcher, leaves the mind in its natural state. It doesn't accept or reject thoughts and emotions. It doesn't create or follow the habitual patterns of thought.

The Dharmakaya is "a state of meditation that is like the continuous flowing of a river, (a state in which one) remains, at all times, without attempting to create or stop anything or trying to develop thoughts or calm them down ..."

Patrul Rinpoche[11]

It seems to me that this difference between yulchen and rigpa is a fundamental difference; it is the fundamental difference between the egocentric and egoless mind. The egoless mind does not accept, reject or follow, but the egocentric mind does.

In addition, this is a way of empirically describing this fundamental differences between the ego and egoless mind. It is a way of describing these differences that is based on and derived from observations the mind.

KTG: Yes.

HMV: Science is about deriving theory from experience. I'm wondering if it would be ok with you to talk about these issues in terms of our actual experience of the mind. Could we discuss these issues by talking about the watcher and the stream of consciousness, and what awareness actually sees as it watches the stream of consciousness go by?

KTG: Yes. But in one way it seems like that when you say "watch your mind," that then there is an object – your mind, and then you are the watcher. So when you say you, the watcher, still it is your mind.

HMV: The mind is watching the mind.

KTG: Yes. The mind is watching the mind.

HMV: It is true that this is dual mind, and that in dual mind, awareness does not recognize that inner appearances[12] are actually manifestations of itself. The watcher of the dual mind sees the inner appearances as being separate from and different than itself. But science believes that the observations it makes with the dual mind are valid.

KTG: Yes. This is dualistic mind. There is a subject and an object. And wherever there is subject and object, there is self. All of the phenomena grasped by the dualistic mind can be understood as having a self.

HMV: All of the grasping is self.

KTG: The grasped phenomena are dag. That is self.

HMV: Suppose the watcher grasps a single thought. Does it attribute a concept of self to that thought?

KTG: Yes.

HMV: Does the watcher then believe that it has the identity, or concept of self, that it has attributed to that thought? For example, suppose my watcher decides that one of my thoughts is a smart thought. Will that simultaneously cause me to believe that I am a smart person? Is that part of the way the ego works?

KTG: Yes. (Emphatic)

HMV: Thank you very much.

Annotation: Please forgive the inclusion of this section. It is, essentially, a presentation by myself of an empirical theory of the differences between the ego and egoless mind. I left it in because it's a set of ideas that the two of us came back to over and again as we continued to talk about the differences between the healthy and unhealthy mind.

THE CAUSE AND NATURE OF SUFFERING

HMV: How does the ego cause suffering?

KTG: By creating ignorance. It is always ignorance that causes suffering.

HMV: How does ignorance create suffering?

KTG: Because it always creates mistakes in the way we see.

HMV: What do you mean by mistakes in the way we see?

KTG: A mistake, for example, would be seeing this table here as a having a self. This is inaccurate; in reality the table does not really exist. It does not have an independent self that has a true existence. Similarly, the grasping of one's own self is a fault. This is also a mistake. Even in the relative sense, if we really investigate or analyze, the self does not exist. When you see yourself, or an object like the table, as having a self, it is a hallucinating consciousness and a hallucinated object. Both are just complete mistakes.

HMV: By mistake, then, you mean an inaccurate way of seeing something.

KTG: Yes.

HMV: It sounds like you are also saying Khenpo, that when the mind grasps itself and thinks that it really exists – I am a doctor, I am a Khenpo, whatever – that it is this grasping that is the cause of suffering. It is this grasping that creates the ego that causes suffering. Is this a fair way to put it?

KTG: Yes.

HMV: Why does the creation and grasping of one's self cause suffering?

KTG: Because when you grasp your self, whether you think you are a Khenpo or a doctor or even if you are just thinking that you are an "I," then based on that, there is attachment; attachment to that concept of self. And then based on that attachment, there arises all of the concepts that reject all of the things that are bad for one's self and grab all of the things that are good for one's self. And by putting so much effort into this process, and by doing lots of wrong actions as a result, then suffering arises. It is based on these causes and conditions.

HMV: So the mind with an ego is forever and always stuck with the full time task of accepting and rejecting its experiences, and it does so on the basis of whether or not they are good or bad for its concept of self.

KTG: Yes. (Emphatic)

Annotation: Khenpo is saying here that when you think you have a self, it causes you to suffer because it causes you to become attached to the concept of self you have created. When you become attached to a concept of your self, you are automatically imposing upon your mind the full time task of judging all of its experiences and all of the meanings[13] that appear in its stream of consciousness. In Khenpo's estimation, you judge them towards the end of rejecting and accepting them on the basis of whether or not they support, or are good for, your concept of self. It's a full time job and a lot of work.

HMV: Thank you. Now let's say, for example, that I have a concept of my self as a happy person. And then let's suppose further that I get angry; that the emotion of anger arises within me. If my watcher rejects that anger because it is inconsistent with my concept of myself as a happy person, is this an example of what you mean by accepting and rejecting experiences on the basis of your self concept?

KTG: When you think of your self as a doctor, and somebody says, "Oh you are not a good doctor," then instantly it affects your ego. You have a concept of your self. You think "I am a good doctor." When you hear the words "not a good doctor," you get affected by them.

HMV: My ego gets affected by just hearing those words "not a good doctor."

KTG: Yes. It gets affected, and then an emotion will arise with that feeling.

HMV: Perhaps the emotion of anger would arise.

KTG: The emotion of anger could arise, or perhaps hatred. Afflicted minds of some kind will definitely arise, and with the afflicted minds, everything we do is the cause of suffering.

HMV: Is it the experience of the emotions of anger and hatred that is the actual suffering?

KTG: Yes. Because the emotions are negative.

HMV: Are they painful?

KTG: Negative. The negative thoughts cause negative actions. The negative thoughts and the negative actions are the cause of suffering. They are always the cause of suffering. When you are angry, for example, you really don't feel happy or comfortable. We can prove that anger is negative because one feels guilty in response. Why does one feel guilty if it is not bad?

HMV: Are you saying that if I act out of anger, that the anger will make me feel guilty, and that the feeling of guilt is the suffering?

KTG: No. The feeling of guilt itself can be either positive or negative. Sometimes, when you do the wrong thing, you feel guilty. You feel sorry for what you did. That can be good. It is the emotion that is negative. When one feels angry, one does not have joy.

HMV: Ah. The anger causes suffering because it blocks out your ability to know and feel the joy that is the nature of the mind.

KTG: Yes.

HMV: And this, then, is why the egocentric mind is not happy.

KTG: Yes. Yes.

HMV: The anger created by the ego blocks out the joy that is the natural state of the mind.

KTG: Yes. (Emphatic)

HMV: So it's like the sun and the clouds.

KTG: Yes. The enotions and thought are obscurations.

HMV: In other words, when the thoughts and emotions of the egocentric mind arise, that they are like clouds. They are clouds in the sense that they block our ability to know and be the sun of rigpa; they block our ability to know the joyful spacious nondual awareness that is always present in our mind. Is that a fair way to put it?

KTG: Yes. Yes.

HMV: Thank you very much.

Annotation: The Khenpo has returned, here, to the question of the natural state of the mind. He is saying, once again, that the natural state of the mind is happiness and joy. In addition, he is now saying that human beings suffer because the emotions and thoughts created by the ego block our ability to know and be this natural joy of the mind. The natural joy of the mind is, like the sun in the sky, always present within the mind. Sometimes, though, it appears as though it is not there because it has been covered over by our thoughts and emotions.

THE HEALTHY MIND IS
THE EGOLESS MIND

HMV: Now let's switch and go over to the healthy side of things. Would you say that the egoless mind is a healthy mind?

KTG: Yes.

HMV: Why do you say that Khenpo?

KTG: Because it is a free mind.

HMV: Free. Does that mean the mind with an ego is not free?

KTG: Not free.

HMV: Why is the mind with an ego not free?

KTG: Because it is dependent on many different causes and conditions. It does not have complete freedom.

HMV: It is not the natural mind.

KTG: Of course it is not the natural mind. It is dependent on causes and conditions. Something that is dependent is like a prison.

HMV: What are the causes and conditions upon which ego depends?

KTG: Your personal karma; all of your habitual tendencies. The ego is something that is not independent.

HMV: Are you saying that the happiness of the egocentric mind is dependent upon the content of the thoughts, emotions and stories it creates? That its feeling of well being is dependent upon them?

KTG: Yes. (Emphatic)[14]

HMV: And that as a result, it is not free of them.

KTG: Yes. (Emphatic)

HMV: Thank you. There also seems to be another way in which the mind with an ego is not free. As you said before, the watcher with an ego is also stuck with the unremitting task of trying to control its stream of consciousness. Instead of having the freedom of simply allowing its stream of consciousness to run free, dissolve and self liberate,[15] it must constantly do the work of monitoring its stream of consciousness.

KTG: Yes. Yes. That's true.

HMV: Thank you. Now you were saying before that the egoless mind is a healthy mind because it is free.

KTG: Yes. It is free. Completely independent and free. It does not have any delusions or emotions. It is free of all of the concepts that are created by the ego. It has only perfected, accomplished and pure qualities.[16]

HMV: Does the egoless mind suffer?

KTG: No. (Emphatic)

HMV: Why not?

KTG: Because there is no cause of suffering.

HMV: And by cause of suffering do you mean karma and the habitual patterns of thought?

KTG: And the ego itself. (Lots of shared laughter)

THE NATURE OF
RIGPA/EGOLESS AWARENESS

HMV: In the same way that we were saying before that the ego is a specific form of self awareness – a specific kind of relationship between the watcher and the stream of consciousness, I wonder if we can talk about the egoless mind in the same way? Can we say that the egoless mind is rang-rig yeshe[17] – a nondual form of self awareness in which the watcher relates to the stream of consciousness in an entirely different way?

KTG: Ok.

Annotation: We have already defined ego as a specific mode of self awareness in which the watcher has dual awareness of the thoughts and emotions that appear in its stream of consciousness because it accepts, rejects and follows those thoughts and emotions. Now I am asking Khenpo if we can define the egoless mind as being a different mode of self awareness; as a different type of relationship between awareness and the stream of consciousness.

HMV: Can we say that egoless awareness is rigpa?

KTG: Yes.

HMV: Can we say that rigpa, unlike yulchen – the watcher of the egocentric mind, is an awareness that does not grasp inner appearances.

KTG: Right.

HMV: And that as a result, everything is different.

KTG: Yes.

HMV: In the mind with an ego, it is the watcher that knows and responds to the thoughts, emotions and habitual patterns of thought. Is rigpa the awareness of the egoless mind?

KTG: Yes.

HMV: What kind of inner appearances is rigpa aware of?

KTG: In relation to awareness, rigpa?

HMV: Yes. What kind of inner appearances appear to rigpa when it knows itself?

KTG: In the field of rigpa there is no subject and object.

HMV: Ok.

KTG: Whatever appears is rigpa itself.

HMV: Right.

KTG: It's just rigpa's display. They are appearanaces of rigpa itself.

HMV: By display, do you mean rigpa tsal?[18]

KTG: Yes. Rigpa tsal. Rigpa realizes the true nature of the inner appearances created by rigpa tsal. Rigpa never ever conceptualizes or clings to itself, and as a result, it never has dual awareness of itself. Whatever appears to rigpa is a pure appearance.[19] At the same time, everything is liberated in its nature. There is no source for the ego. It is completely egoless. Rigpa is always in that moment where there are no conceptual thoughts. It is pure and perfected.

Relatively, we say that the experience of rigpa is pure and perfected, but still the actual experience of rigpa can not be expressed in words. Awareness and the actual realization of the true nature of mind are inconceivable by our present mind. There is no language that we can use to express that experience.

"Realization of the absolute nature is like the dream of a mute."

Padampa Sangye [20]

There is, to be sure, some kind of result or fruition that one can and does experience in realization, but there is no language or example that we can use to put that experience into a relative communication that another person could understand. Nonetheless, it can be said that rigpa is pure or perfect, without concepts. It is just completely free, completely liberated, omniscient mind.

HMV: So if you use words, or concepts, to describe the experiences of rigpa, then it becomes dual mind. Then it is the same thing as ego because the essence of grasping is imputing a concept of self to an appearance.

KTG: Yes.

HMV: If we talk about the experience of rigpa by imputing concepts to it, it's no longer rigpa. Is this not what you mean?

KTG: Yes. (Emphatic) Rigpa and using concepts are two different things.

HMV: Oh yes.

KTG: Using concepts to understand rigpa is just the relative method of describing rigpa. But there is no way we can describe rigpa itself with any sort of concepts. That is why it is said to be inconceivable and inconceivable in its nature.

HMV: Understood. You know, in our previous conversations five years ago, we talked about nonconceptual mind (tog-may shespa).

KTG: Yes.

HMV: And at that time you said that the nonconceptual mind is a kind of wisdom awareness.

KTG: Yes.

HMV: You said that it is like space…

KTG: Yes.

HMV: That it has no boundaries…

KTG: Yes. (Emphatic)

HMV: That it is joyous. Blissful.

KTG: Um hm.

HMV: And has nondual awareness of all phenomena.

KTG: Yes. (Emphatic)

HMV: Is this nonconceptual mind the same thing as rigpa?

KTG: The same.

HMV: Ok. So it is possible, then, to describe the qualities of rigpa in this way. We can say this much about rigpa.

KTG: Yes.

HMV: But we can't actually describe the experience that rigpa is having without turning it into dual mind. Is that a fair distinction?

KTG: Yes.

Annotation: We have made a distinction here. Earlier, Khenpo said that it is not possible to describe the content of nondual, or egoless, experiences. Here he is saying that despite the fact that it is not possible to depict these experiences, it **is** possible describe the qualities of the awareness that is having those experiences. It can be said, for example, that rigpa is like space, has no boundaries, is joyous, is nonconceptual and has nondual awareness of all phenomena.

It should not be forgotten, however, that even though it is possible to articulate the qualities of rigpa, it would be a definite mistake to set those qualities up as goals to be attained in meditation:

*With natural abiding, there is nothing for
anyone to contrive.
To abide in what simply is, without its being
sought,
means that nothing need be done – this is
revealed to be
the most sublime activity.*

The All Creating Monarch[21]

HMV: Fair enough. Now can we also say,
thank you, that rigpa is aware of inner
appearances?

KTG: Yes.

HMV: Can rigpa be aware of yeshe, nondual
primordial wisdom, as an inner appearance?
Is that possible?

KTG: Yes. Sure. Relatively we can say that.

HMV: We can say it happens, but, we're not
describing the experience itself.

KTG: Yes.

HMV: Can rigpa be aware of a predual inner appearance, or gzhi-nang?[22]

KTG: Yes.

HMV: Thank you. Can rigpa be aware of the three different types of nyams?[23]

KTG: Yes.

HMV: Can rigpa ever be aware of a realization, or nyams dang togs-pa?

KTG: Once again, in a relative way of understanding, we can say that. Yes.

HMV: But ultimately we could not say that.

KTG: Yes. We could not say it exactly like that because the realization is not separate from rigpa.

THE TWO MODES OF
SELF AWARENESS

HMV: Thank you very much. Now, I'd like to take a systematic look at the differences between the watcher and rigpa. For one, it seems that the egocentric watcher grasps thoughts, emotions and bag-chags, whereas rigpa, egoless awareness, does not grasp any of the appearances that arise before it.

KTG: No. Not at all.

HMV: This seems to me to be one of the primary differences between the watcher and rigpa. Would you agree?

KTG: Yes. It's a big difference.

HMV: Why is that a big difference?

KTG: Because they are two completely different natures. One is the relative nature, and one is the absolute nature.

HMV: And one causes suffering and the other doesn't.

KTG: Oh yes. In rigpa, which is the absolute truth, sems ...

HMV: Dual mind...

KTG: Yes. In rigpa, dual mind does exist at all. Dual mind is just exactly like a hallucination and a hallucinated object. Dual mind is not perceived by a Buddha, and dual mind does not have true nature. So in the ultimate sense, it does not even exist; the ego and the dual mind and all the deluded minds do not really exist.

HMV: Not only do they not exist; they do not even appear.

KTG: Yes.

HMV: Do bag-chags ever appear to rigpa?
KTG: No.

HMV: Do thoughts ever appear to rigpa
KTG: No.

HMV: Do emotions ever appear to rigpa?
KTG: No. It's not possible.

HMV: And why isn't it possible?
KTG: Again, because they are a different nature.

HMV: Is it because there is no grasping?
KTG: Yes. There's no grasping.

HMV: Would it be correct to say that because there's no grasping, that thoughts don't arise.
KTG: Yes.

HMV: And that because there's no grasping, emotions don't arise.

KTG: Yes.

HMV: And because there's no grasping the bag-chags don't arise.

KTG: Yes. We can say it in that way.

Annotation: In this last series of questions, Khenpo Tsewang takes the definite position that thoughts and emotions never appear to rigpa – nondual egoless awareness. I have heard many other lamas take this exact same position as well. I have also heard many lamas take the opposite position – that thoughts and emotions do appear to and are known by rigpa. Khenpo Tsewang, himself, takes this position at a later point in this book.

This is an important issue. Why? Because it presents us with two very different pictures of the healthy mind; two very different pictures of egoless awareness, or rigpa.

If, on the one hand, the egoless mind is a mind that never experiences thoughts and emotions, then this would seem to mean that a healthy mind is a mind that suppresses all of its thoughts and emotions. It would also mean that the healthy mind would have to be defined as a mind in which thoughts and emotions do not appear.

If, on the other hand, rigpa, the egoless mind, is an awarenss to which thoughts and emotions do appear, then this would present us with a very different picture of the healthy mind. This type of egoless mind would not suppress thoughts and emotions. It would, in contrast, be a mind that is totally open to the appearance of thoughts and emotions; a mind that would allow thoughts and emotions to remain in their natural state and dissolve into the nondual mind they have always been.

Here's one opinion on the matter as stated in "The Six Expanses," a text cited by Longchenpa in his "Treasure Trove of Scriptural Transmission."[24] The passage describes "mind itself" – another name for nondual mind:

*Within mind itself, there are conceptual
frameworks:
Myriad appearances arise naturally,
And so, with their individual names and colors,
They are perfect in the dualistic way they
manifest as forms.*

*Within mind itself, there is what can be
transformed:
Afflictive emotions arise naturally,
And so, like poison being transformed into
medicine
They are perfect as the epitome of the kayas and
timeless awareness.*

*Within mind itself, there is what can be freed:
Sense objects manifest as they do,
And so, being like a knot in a snake that
releases itself,
They are free and perfect in their own place.*

Longchenpa summarizes this passage by saying that awareness is "... far from ... being ... nonexistent, like some kind of void; it is called 'great perfection,' because both the true nature of phenomena and the phenomena themselves are perfect as the essence of both the two levels of truth and the three aspects of purity."

Ultimately, I would like to think that this is an empirical issue. It seems entirely possible that a group of people who have experienced the egoless mind could sit down together and compare their observations of that experience. They could do so in much the same way that physicists compare their observations of galaxies and elementary particles. Once this has been done, it should then be feasible to determine which of these two hypotheses is correct. My own opinion is that once this discussion has been held, we will find that there is a sense in which both of these hypotheses are correct.

HMV: A quick aside now. Who is it, in the mind, that thinks it has an identity? In other words, in the mind with an ego, who is it that is actually thinking that it has a self concept? Take me for example, Hank. If I think I have an identity, who is it that is thinking that? Is it the watcher?

KTG: Of course, relatively speaking it is the watcher.

HMV: It is the watcher then, my watcher, that thinks it has a self.

KTG: Yes. (Emphatic)

HMV: And then, because it thinks it has a self, it behaves as though it has a self to protect. It accepts, rejects, and follows.

KTG: Yes.

HMV: Now does rigpa think it has a self?

KTG: No. (Emphatic)

HMV: Is this another important difference between the watcher and rigpa?

KTG: Yes.

HMV: Between egocentric mind and egoless mind.

KTG: Yes.

HMV: Does rigpa behave differently than the watcher because it doesn't think it has a self?

KTG: Yes. (Emphatic) Completely different.

HMV: I'd like to summarize. I think that we have mapped out some of the defining differences between rigpa and the watcher. We've established that rigpa is egoless awareness, that the watcher is egocentric awareness, and the two of them are very different.

KTG: Yes. Very different.

HMV: And I think we have described the essential differences between the two. The watcher believes it has an identity.

KTG: Yes.

HMV: And as a result, it accepts, rejects and follows its thoughts and emotions; and it suffers.

KTG: Yes.

HMV: And rigpa, or egoless awareness, doesn't believe it has an identity.

KTG: Yes.

HMV: And as a result, it does not grasp any of the inner appearances that it knows.

KTG: Yes.

HMV: Which means that those remain pure. They remain pure in the sense that they do not change into conceptual, or dual, appearances.

KTG: Yes.

HMV: And as a result, rigpa does not suffer.
KTG: Yes.

Annotation: Here, then, is the essential and defining difference between the ego and the egoless mind. They are two different forms of self awareness. They are, respectively, dual self awareness and nondual self awareness:

There is simply realization or its lack within the realm of
the basic space of phenomena.
For those with realization, who have reached a state of bliss,
there is pure perception.
For those without it, there is nonrecognition of awareness
and the habitual patterns of dualistic perception,
from which sensory appearances manifest in all their variety,
though none of this strays from basic space.

Longchenpa[25]

HMV: These, then, are the basic differences between egocentric and egoless awareness.

KTG: Yes. But at the same time, rigpa and the ultimate nature are always there without it being decreased or increased.

HMV: It's always there.

KTG: Yes. It's always there. Right now and always. It doesn't change.

HMV: That's the beauty of it. Because all you have to do is stop grasping your own mind.

KTG: Yes. Just recognize the rigpa. Right now. All of this ego grasping is mistaken and confused. All of the concepts and phenomena are confused.

HMV: You can just stop believing in all of that stuff in an instant, can't you?

KTG: Yes. The moment we recognize the true nature of our mind, all this confusion just disappears by itself.

REALIZING THE TRUE NATURE OF THOUGHTS

HMV: When you say recognize the true nature of your mind, do you mean recognize the true nature of your thoughts? The true nature of rigpa? Or both?

KTG: Actually, I mean recognize rigpa. But in the Dzog-Chen practice, there is a practice in which you can realize the true nature of thoughts.

HMV: What practice is that?

KTG: DzogChen meditation.

HMV: Do you mean trekcho?[26]

KTG: Yes. Trekcho.

HMV: What does it mean to recognize the true nature of thoughts?

KTG: You recognize that the thought is a thought, and then you don't pursue that thought.

HMV: I see. Not following the thoughts.

KTG: Yes.

HMV: Are you saying that if you do not follow your thoughts, that you are recognizing their nature?

KTG: Yes.

HMV: Is that the same thing as recognizing the emptiness of your thoughts?

KTG: Yes. You can say it like that.

HMV: How can you tell inside yourself that you are actually not following your thoughts? What are the indications that you are not pursuing your thoughts?

KTG: If one's own mind is not obscured to one's self, then you are not following your thoughts.

HMV: Ahh. Do you mean that the thoughts of my dual mind are not obscured to my watcher?

KTG: Yes. (Emphatic)

HMV: Ok. If you are having clear awareness of your thoughts, then you can be certain that you are not following them.

KTG: Yes. Then you know that you are recognizing your thoughts, and that you are not following them.

HMV: What's the Tibetan word that you are using, here, for thought?

KTG: Thought is rnam-tog.

HMV: Ok. We're talking about ordinary dualistic thoughts.

KTG: Yes. Then it is ok. There is no problem.

HMV: But if you react as if your mind is not ok — by accepting, rejecting, judging and following – that makes it seem as though it is not ok.

KTG: Yes.

HMV: As soon as we stop all of that, then lo and behold, it's all ok.

KTG: Yes. It's ok.

HMV: It's a kind of a miracle.

HOW THE WATCHER
BECOMES RIGPA

HMV: Now once again, in the mind's dual experience of itself, it seems as though there is both a stream of consciousness and an awareness that is watching the stream of consciousness.

KTG: That's possible. At a subtle level. Yes.

HMV: Why is that subtle?

KTG: Because normally we don't experience our mind in that way.

HMV: How do we experience our mind normally?

KTG: Normally, we don't experience all of our thoughts. Sometimes thoughts arise, and you don't notice them. The thoughts just happen. But when you concentrate in meditation, you become more aware of your thoughts.

HMV: And this, then, is the experience that we all have in meditation where you experience yourself as having an involuntary stream of consciousness and as being a watcher that is watching the stream of consciousness.

KTG: Yes.

HMV: It sounds like you are saying that this experience is actually a skill that has to be developed; that seeing your mind as having an awareness that is separate from your stream of consciousness is a developed skill.

KTG: Yes. It develops as a result of looking into the mind based on these practices, and it is good to develop this kind of awareness.

HMV: Would it be fair to say that this is a first or second step towards the development of egoless mind? Is that what you are saying?

KTG: Yes.

HMV: Because, after all, this is still dual mind.

KTG: Yes.

HMV: If we went walking outside right now and stopped the first person we saw and asked that person if they have, in their mind, a watcher that is looking at their stream of consciousness, do you think they would say yes or no?

KTG: They would say no.

HMV: (laughter) Ok. So that really is what you mean. The experience of having a watcher is something that is created by the practice of meditation.

KTG: Yes.

HMV: Thank you.

KTG: Those who are trained to watch their mind, they have this kind of experience. Normal people don't.

HMV: Is it helpful to develop this kind of experience?

KTG: Yes.

HMV: Why?

KTG: Because this experience is a step towards realizing the nature of mind.

HMV: Are you saying that it is the watcher that realizes the nature of mind?

KTG: Yes. (Emphatic)

HMV: How does the watcher realize the nature of mind?

KTG: It happens if the watcher knows what the mind looks like, what its actual characteristics are, where the thoughts come from and how they arise. That way you can go much deeper into it, and then you can get into the nakedness of the nature of mind.

"When abandoning the watcher in awareness itself, there is utter emptiness free from color and shape."
                            Chokgyur Lingpa[27]

HMV: Would it be fair to say, then, that meditation creates the watcher?

KTG: Yes.

HMV: Would it also be fair to say that meditation creates the watcher so that eventually the watcher can realize the nature of the mind?

KTG: Yes.

HMV: So that eventually the watcher can realize the emptiness of the mind?

KTG: Yes.

HMV: Does this mean that eventually the egocentric watcher is transformed into egoless awareness, or rigpa?

KTG: Yes.

HMV: How does the watcher become egoless awareness?

KTG: At the moment that it recognizes the true nature of mind.

HMV: When the watcher recognizes the true nature of mind, then it becomes rigpa.

KTG: Yes.

HMV: Thank you very much.

KTG: When it realizes that there is no mind and there is no watcher, then it is realizing the truth.

HMV: When you say that the watcher realizes there really is no mind or watcher, what exactly do you mean?

KTG: Normally we think that there is a mind and we think there is a second mind that is watching it. When we think in this way, it seems like there is a duality of subject and object. But in reality this duality does not really exist in this way. So then at some point it dissolves. The subjective and objective aspect of that mind becomes nondual.

HMV: Ahh. The watcher becomes rigpa when it realizes nondual mind.

KTG: Yes.

HMV: And is that also what you mean by realizing the truth?

KTG: Yes. There is no subject or object existing any more.

HMV: In other words, when the mind realizes rang-rig yeshe, nondual self awareness, it is realizing the truth. This is the truth.

KTG: Yes.

Annotation: The watcher of the ego mind becomes the egoless watcher, rigpa, when it realizes nondual mind. The healthy, or egoless, mind **is** the mind that has nondual awareness of itself – rang-rig yeshe.

HMV: And this is the same as the watcher having nondual awareness of itself; the same as rigpa having nondual awareness of itself.

KTG: Yes.

HMV: Would it be correct to say that when the watcher realizes the emptiness of the stream of consciousness, that it is having nondual awareness of the stream of consciousness.

KTG: Yes.

HMV: And is this the same thing as realizing the truth?

KTG: Yes.

HMV: Thank you very much

EXPERIENCING THE NATURE OF MIND

HMV: At this point, I'd like to play back to you a tiny portion of an interview that we did before and ask you some questions about that passage.

KTG: Ok.

> *HMV: Can a tog-may, or non-conceptual thought, appear in an egoless mind?*
>
> *KTG: A tog-may is a direct perception. The direct perception itself is a kind of awareness. That kind of awareness itself is the nature of mind. And that itself is the wisdom.*

> *HMV: The wisdom is the awareness itself.*
>
> *KTG: Yes.*

HMV: Not the appearances?

KTG: Not the appearances.

HMV: Just the awareness.

KTG: Yes. The awareness itself is the wisdom. And the wisdom itself is clarity. And clarity itself is there from the beginning. It never dissolves. It never develops and it never decreases.

HMV: If you are asleep is that clarity present?

KTG: Yes.

HMV: If you are knocked unconscious, is that same wisdom present?

KTG: The wisdom is there.

HMV: Can you describe what that awareness is like? Is there any way you can describe the experience of that awareness?

KTG: *It's like space. It does not have an end. It does not have a beginning. It does not have borders.*

HMV: *Does that space-like awareness have a blissful quality to it.*

KTG: *Yes. Definitely.*

HMV: *Does it have any other qualities?*

KTG: *Clarity.*

HMV: *By clarity do you mean that there are no thoughts?*

KTG: *Yes. No thoughts.*

HMV: *Is that spacious, blissful and clear wisdom awareness aware of inner appearances?*

KTG: *It is aware of all phenomena, but it is never gasping or clinging or involved in them.*

HMV: *That's very clear. (Laughter)*

HMV: Now a few questions about this passage. And thank you.

KTG: Ok.

HMV: When the mind is abiding in this spacious and blissful awareness, do all of the inner appearances that arise in the mind dissolve?

KTG: Inner appearances? Do you mean like thoughts and feelings?

HMV: Yes.

KTG: If one has the actual meditation practice, then they all dissolve.

HMV: In my own experience, it feels like the bliss is actually dissolving the thoughts or inner appearances. It just seems like the bliss is melting them away as they arise, like a flame would melt butter.

KTG: Hm.

HMV: Is that your experience as well? Does the bliss actually work to dissolve the thoughts?

KTG: The actual antidote that dissolves the thoughts is the nature of mind itself – which is actually a combination of emptiness, clarity and the great compassion. When one has a strong experience of bliss, one can not experience any of the minor thoughts.[28] So that is why it appears like the bliss is dissolving the thoughts.

HMV: Are you saying that when the bliss that is the nature of the mind is present, that thoughts can't appear in the mind?

KTG: Yes.

HMV: Why can't thoughts appear when that blissful awareness is present in the mind?

KTG: Because the thoughts arise in the form of bliss. We know the thoughts, but we do not identify with them.

"Worldly thoughts are realized as Dharmakaya. So the natural great bliss arises within. There is no need of acceptance and rejection since all phenomena arise as the lama."

Longchenpa[29]

HMV: No identifying. No grasping. No accepting, no rejecting.

KTG: Yes.

HMV: And that's why they dissolve.

KTG: Yes.

HMV: When that bliss is there as awareness, the mind doesn't grasp, accept, or reject. It just allows everything to remain in its natural state.

KTG: Yes.

HMV: Is that actually your experience, too?

KTG: Yes.

HMV: Thank you. It also seems like this bliss just naturally emerges or arises as the thoughts disappear. In other words, you don't have to make it come. In fact, you can't make it come. It comes naturally on its own as the thoughts slow down and dissolve.

KTG: Yes.

HMV: Is that your experience?

KTG: Oh yes. The fountain rises.

HMV: But you can't make the fountain rise, can you; even if you tried all day or all of your life? It can only come naturally.

KTG: That's right.

HMV: Because they haven't been grasped.

KTG: Yes.

HMV: Could this wisdom awareness also be called gzhi?[31]

KTG: Yes. According to DzogChen.

HMV: Thank you. Can it be called chos-ku?[32]

KTG: Yes.

HMV: Thank you. Is the purpose of meditation to develop this space-like and blissful awareness?

KTG: The purpose of meditation is to just to recognize the nature of mind, and to maintain it.

HMV: And it sounds like you are saying that the nature of mind is this blissful space-like awareness.

KTG: Yes.

HMV: Would if be fair to say, then, that what meditation does is train the mind to stop grasping, rejecting, accepting, following; and that as a result of this training the mind realizes the nature of mind which is a blissful and clear space-like awareness?

KTG: Yes.

HMV: Thank you very much.

Ah! In supreme bliss – just as it is, effortless –
Do not make any effort with body,
speech or mind.
Do not contrive or create constructs.
Do not conceptualize.
Do not be influenced by the
characteristics of things.
Rest in the ultimate experience of bliss,
naturally occurring
timeless awareness.

The All Creating Monarch[33]

CONCEPTUAL AND NONCONCEPTUAL JOY

HMV: Just a few more questions now. My experience is that when I stop grasping – when I stop accepting, rejecting, judging and following my thoughts – that my thoughts slow down. The waves of the ocean start to disappear. The thoughts slow down more and more, and as they continue to slow down, a feeling of joy arises within me, and then as that feeling grows, it becomes more and more stable and then it becomes me.

KTG: Aha!

HMV: You know what I mean.

KTG: Yes.

HMV: It becomes me in the sense that it becomes my awareness – the awareness that knows my inner and outer world. Sometimes it comes. Sometimes it goes. When it is present, all of the inner appearances that arise in the face of that joy dissolve and disappear. Do you know this experience? Is this an experience that occurs on the path?

KTG: It can happen. But there can be conceptual joy and non-conceptual joy.

HMV: What is the difference between conceptual joy and non-conceptual joy?

KTG: Conceptual joy is experiencing the joy and then having the concept that this is joy: "Oh this is so good." This is conceptual joy.

HMV: In other words, you become aware that you are in a good state of mind, and you label it as such.

KTG: Yes.

HMV: Which would make you want to hold onto this joyous awareness, and as a result it would become, in turn, a form of ego.

KTG: Yes. Yes.

HMV: Then what is non-conceptual joy?

KTG: Non-conceptual joy is the opposite of that. You have the joy, but you have no concept of it at all.

HMV: You don't step back from it and go "Aha, this is good."

KTG: Yes.

HMV: You just are the nondual joy.

KTG: Yes. The joy and one's self are not separate. It is like the first moment of the tongue tasting chocolate. When the sweetness of the chocolate and the subject meet, there is a sense of knowing the taste without any concepts.

*When awareness is a space that leaves the stream
of consciousness in its natural state,
When awareness ceases to believe and live in the
ego narratives created by the stream of
consciousness,
the thoughts and emotions of the mind
dissolve and become joy.
The joy that is space-like nondual self awareness.
The joy that is the natural state of your mind.*

APPENDIX

SELF-LIBERATION

HMV: On another occasion you once said that if you recognize the nature of your thoughts, they will self-liberate into wisdom.

KTG: Ok.

HMV: When a thought self-liberates into wisdom, does it dissolve?

KTG: Yes.

HMV: Is that a moment of non-dual awareness?

KTG: Yes.

HMV: Thank you. Now suppose an angry thought arises, the mind recognizes its nature, the anger dissolves and mirror like wisdom appears. Would that be an example of the self-liberation of a thought?

KTG: Yes.

HMV: Suppose a hundred thoughts dissolve. Will each of those thoughts turn into a non-dual wisdom, or just some of them?

KTG: In general there are many sub-thoughts[34] and not each of the sub-thoughts will necessarily change into wisdom.

HMV: In other words, it's not the case that each and every sub-thought will turn into wisdom.

KTG: Yes. What happens is that all the thoughts disappear and then there is one wisdom.

HMV: Ahh.

KTG: And that wisdom has one nature and different features. Yes. There is one wisdom, but that wisdom can appear as mirror-like wisdom or sameness wisdom. It's like that. One nature. Five aspects.

HMV: Ok. Those are the five wisdoms.[35]
KTG: Yes.

HMV: I'd like to make sure that I've understood you. It sounds like you are saying that one kind of transformation that can happen to a stream of thoughts when many many thoughts are going through your mind …
KTG: Yes.

HMV: … is that all of a sudden that stream of thoughts will dissolve and one wisdom will appear in their place.
KTG: Yes.

HMV: Does that wisdom remain present for a short time or a long time?

KTG: That depends on the practitioner. Actually it is always there in the ordinary mind, but it is just not always recognized.

HMV: Ok.

KTG: But once your practice is stabilized, it appears for a longer time.

HMV: Ok. Does that wisdom appear as a single appearance, or phenomenon, in the stream of consciousness, or does it appear as a specific type of awareness?

KTG: As a type of awareness.

THE EGOLESS EGO OF THE BODHISATTVA

HMV: I'd like to turn, now, to another issue. In doing these lama interviews, and in particular with you, I think I've come to an understanding that I wanted to run by you and see if you think it is correct. When we were talking about accepting and rejecting thoughts earlier on, you said that you would reject the thought of stealing. Or accept the thought of compassion.

KTG: Yes.

HMV: That this is actually part of your path.

KTG: Yes.

according to the Sutrayana, and the DzogChen path is one on which you don't accept, reject, follow and so forth. But for one particular person, these two different paths become stages. First you do the Hinayana way of practice, then the Bodhisattva way of practice. Then it goes higher and higher, and then comes the DzogChen practice.

HMV: Does the bodhisattva practice of accepting and rejecting thoughts interfere with the DzogChen practice of not accepting, rejecting and following? I can see that you know what I am going to ask and that your answer is going to be no.

KTG: That's right. Someone who is practicing DzogChen is also on the Bodhisattva path.

HMV: At the same time.

KTG: Yes. It is not separate from the DzogChen path. If the DzogChen path is totally separate from the Bodhisattva path then that is not the actual DzogChen.

HMV: So I'm still wondering how they go together, since they seem to involve different ways of relating to one's own mind. In thinking about this issue, here is what occurs to me. I'd like to find out if you think it's right or wrong.

I think that at first, a DzogChen practitioner would try to be a bodhisattva and reject and accept thoughts on that basis. At some point, though, you transcend the bodhi-sattva ego, and then you would stop rejecting, accepting and following your thoughts and emotions. So you are still trying to be a bodhisattva, but you are also allowing your thoughts to remain in their natural state. Is that how it works?

KTG: Yes. The actual meditation practice for one's self is to apply the DzogChen path, which is, as you know, the fastest path in meditation. That whatever thought arises, you just recognize it and let it go. Then on the bodhisattva path, there are positive thoughts and negative thoughts. To reject negative thoughts and accept positive thoughts is more for relating to sentient beings. It's the external practice.

HMV: Oh. So you divide it up. On the inside with your mind you do DzogChen.

KTG: Yes; in your meditation practice.

HMV: But in your day to day life, you continue to try and be a bodhisattva and accept and reject.

KTG: Yes.

HMV: Very Interesting. (Lots of laughter)

KTG: For example, suppose a thought of desire comes. According to DzogChen, there is nothing to accept or reject. But it is also a danger to the practitioner who does not understand what it really means to say there is nothing to accept, nothing to reject. So they start doing things thinking that a bad thought is nothing to reject. Then there is the possibility of creating negative karma. So on the bodhisattva path one must reject a thought that is the cause of negative karma.

HMV: So are you saying that on the DzogChen path you would reject the thought of desire for another human being?

KTG: No. On the DzogChen path you don't reject thoughts. When a negative thought arises, you just recognize it and let it dissolve.

Footnotes

1   The Tibetan term that we were using for ego here was dag-dzin. Several aspects of the meaning of this term will be explored and explained as the interview progresses.

2   Chandrakirti and Santideva were both seminal Buddhist philosophers who lived in India in the second half of the first millennium A.D.

3   The essence of samsara is suffering. In Buddhism, the term samsara, or cyclic existence, has both cosmological and psychological meaning. It can refer to either a literal place in the mythological universe of Buddhism where beings lead lives of suffering, for example the animal realm; or it can refer to an egocentric state of mind in which people lead lives of suffering.

4   The "nature of the mind" is another name for the egoless, or natural, mind. We will be discussing the nature of mind at length throughout the entire book.

5   Here the Khenpo is taking the classic Mahayana Buddhist position that there are, in the universe, two different kinds of ego, or self. Ultimately, in Buddhist philosophy, the self is just a concept that the mind with an ego attributes to either: (a) a person – by attributing a concept of self to a person or (b) all of the other phenomena that exist in the universe.

It's worth taking a moment to mention here that the translation of the Tibetan term "dag", and its Sanskrit equivalent "atman", has been fraught with some confusion. Both terms have been translated by western scholars into English as both "self" and "ego." As a result, these English terms are often used interchangeably; as the Khenpo and I will be doing throughout the interview.

The confusion comes from the fact that in western thought, the terms "ego" and "self" are not at all equivalent. They have very different meanings. Consider, for example the different meanings of these terms in Jung's work, or

although it has received a number of other translations. Empirically, rigpa is the awareness that knows and is the egoless, or nondual, mind.

11 Reynolds, John M. 1996. The Golden Letters. Ithaca, New York: Snow Lion, pg. 51.

12 The term "inner appearances" is a translation of the Tibetan term "nang-gyi nangwa." There are three different types of appearance, or meaning, that can and do appear in the mind. The term "nang-gyi nangwa" is used here to refer to all of three of those categories. This would include: (a) dual meanings – thoughts and emotions (b) predual meanings – the gzhi-nang, and (c) nondual meanings – yeshe and realizations. For more on the nature of the gzhi-nang, see footnote #22.

13 I am using the term "meaning" here to refer to any construct that the mind creates to give meaning to its sensory experience of the world. That would include thoughts, feelings, emotions, gzhi-nang, yeshe and realizations. To

my eye, the structure of the mind's basic experience of itself is one in which there is: (a) a stream of consciousness in which different kinds of meanings appear and flow by and (b) an awareness that knows and responds to those meanings.

14 For a more thorough discussion of this notion of ego narratives, please see the first book in this series: The Healthy Mind Interviews: Khenpo Nyima Wangyal.

15 Self-liberation is a technical term in DzogChen mind science. It refers to a specific phenomenon. Self liberation occurs when the mind has nondual awareness of a meaning that appears in the stream of consciousness. When the mind has nondual awareness of a meaning, that meaning dissolves and becomes a moment of nondual, or egoless, mind. This is self-liberation.

16 Khenpo is using the term "pure" here to say that only "nondual, or nonconceptual, appearances" arise in the egoless mind.

17 Rang-rig yeshe is a Tibetan term that translates literally as "the self awareness that is primordial wisdom." Empirically, it is nondual self awareness.

18 Rigpa tsal is the "dynamic energy" of rigpa. DzogChen theory says that it is the energy that creates all of the inner appearances of which the mind is aware. Khenpo is saying here that the inner appearances of which rigpa is aware are not separate from rigpa, even though they appear to be. They are appear-ances that are the images in a crystal in a mirror.

In a technical sense, rigpa tsal is translated into English as "dynamic energy." It is a technical term in DzogChen theory that has both metaphysical and psychological meaning. The DzogChen metaphysic takes the position that all of the phenomena we know and perceive are created by rigpa tsal. Rigpa tsal is seen as an energy that is both an expression of rigpa and the source of all phenomena in the universe. In Longchenpa's words:

"Mind itself is a vast expanse, the realm of unchanging space…

Everything is the adornment of basic space and nothing else.

Outwardly and inwardly, things proliferating and resolving are

the dynamic energy of awakened mind."

A Treasure Trove of Scriptural Transmission

[19] Khenpo is using the term "pure appearance" here to mean "nondual, or nonconceptual, appearances."

[20] From Dilgo Khyentse Rinpoche's commentary to "The Hundred Verses of Advice" by Padampa Sangye. Buddhadharma, Summer 2003, pp. 16-23.

[21] As found on page 80 of "A Treasure Trove of Scriptural Transmissions." (see footnote # 31)

[22] Here I am asking khenpo if nondual self awareness can ever be ever aware of the predual meanings that are known as gzhi-nang in DzogChen.

A gzhi-nang is a technical term, in DzogChen mind science, for a type of meaning that can appear in the stream of consciousness. It is a meaning that is simultaneously dual and nondual. Thus it is predual.

A gzhi-snang is dual in the sense that it is an appearance that appears to be separate from the watcher. It is nondual in the sense that it has not yet been grasped by the watcher.

Once it appears, the mind can have either dual or nondual awareness of a gzhi-nang. If the mind has dual awareness of a gzhi-ang, it becomes dual mind. If the mind has nondual awareness of a gzhi-nang, it is transformed into a nondual, or egoless, meaning.

A gzhi-nang, then, is a meaning that appears in the stream of consciousness before it has been transformed into ego or nondual wisdom.

23 The Tibetan term "nyams" is usually translated into English as the term "experience" or "meditative experience." Empirically, it is a moment of nondual awareness.

[24] Longchen Rabjam. 2001. "A Treasure Trove of Scriptural Transmission." Translated under the direction of His Eminence Chagdud Tulku Rinpoche by Richard Barron. Junction City: Padma Publishing, pp. 67-8.

[25] Ibid. pg. 86.

[26] There are two meditation techniques that are unique to DzogChen. One of them is called Trekcho – which is usually translated into English as "cutting through," as in cutting through solid states of mind.

[27] As quoted in "Guidebook for the Bardo" by Choskyi Nyima. Rangjung Yeshe Publications, pg. 78

[28] There are six systematic psychologies in the history of Buddhist ideas. The first systematic psychology is known as the Abhidharma. In the abhidharmic analysis of the mind, there are primary thoughts (sems) and minor thoughts (sems-byung).

[29] Longchen Rabjam. 1989. "Naturally Liberated Mind, The Great Perfection." In The Practice of

DzogChen. Tulku Thondup. Ithaca, NY: Snow Lion Publications, pg. 320.

30 As quoted in Dudjom Rinpoche, "Richo." pg.8

31 Gzhi is another name for egoless awareness. It is the empty awareness that is the ground of all existence.

32 Chosku is yet another name for egoless awareness. It is the Tibetan translation of the Sanskrit term dharmakaya. One of the traditional ways of describing the mind of the Buddha is to describe it as having three aspects: dharmakaya, sambhogakaya and nirmana-kaya. In DzogChen, the dharmakaya is simply the blissful space-like awareness that realizes the emptiness of all phenomena. In this series of questions, after establishing that blissful space-like nondual self awareness is the natural state of the mind, I am asking the Khenpo if dharmakaya is another name for this awareness.

33 From Longchen Rabjam, 2001. "A Treasure Trove of Scriptural Transmission." Translated

under the direction of His Eminence Chagdud Tulku Rinpoche by Richard Barron. Junction City: Padma Publishing, pg. 242.

[34] "Sub-thoughts" is another translation of sems-byung. See footnote #28.

[35] It is traditionally said in Tibetan Buddhism that there are five different primordial, or timeless, wisdoms, each of which corresponds to, and is a nondual transformation of, one of the five basic emotions.

[36] The paramitas are definitive practices of the aspiring bodhisattva.